Count Your Way through
Brazil

by Jim Haskins and Kathleen Benson

illustrations by Liz Brenner Dodson

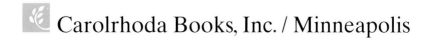
Carolrhoda Books, Inc. / Minneapolis

To Margaret Emily

This book is available in two editions:
Library binding by Carolrhoda Books, Inc.
Soft cover by First Avenue Editions
c/o The Lerner Publishing Group
241 First Avenue North
Minneapolis, MN 55401 U.S.A.

Website address: www.lernerbooks.com

LIBRARY OF CONGRESS CATALOGING-IN-PUBLICATION DATA

Haskins, James.
  Count your way through Brazil / Jim Haskins and
Kathleen Benson ; illustrations by Liz Brenner Dodson.
    p. cm.
  Summary: Uses the Portuguese words for the numbers
from one to ten to introduce the land, history, and
culture of Brazil.
  ISBN 0-87614-873-9 (lib. bdg.)
  ISBN 0-87614-971-9 (pbk.)
  1. Brazil—Civilization—Juvenile literature. 2. Por-
tuguese language—Numerals—Juvenile literature. 3.
Counting—Juvenile literature. [1. Brazil. 2. Counting.]
I. Benson, Kathleen. II. Dodson, Liz Brenner, ill. III.
Title.
F2510.H38 1996
[E]—dc20
[98]   95-43209

Manufactured in the United States of America
2 3 4 5 6 7 –SP – 04 03 02 01 00 99

Introductory Note

Brazil is the fifth largest country in the world and is almost as big as the United States. It is by far the largest nation in Latin America, which includes South America, Central America, Mexico, and the West Indies. Brazil also has one of the largest populations in the world, with more than 150 million people.

It is difficult to make general statements about Brazil because the country is so large and covers so many different kinds of land. One statement that *is* easy to make is that the official language over all those square miles and among all those people is Portuguese.

The Portuguese language has its roots in Latin and is similar to Spanish. Portuguese and Spanish were once even more similar, but they grew apart as they developed in two different countries—Portugal and Spain—with two different histories. Portuguese explorers brought their language to Brazil in the 1500s. Over time, the addition of new words from native Indian and African languages and new forms of pronunciation created a version of Portuguese that is unique to Brazil.

1 um (oong)

Brazil is the **one** nation in South America where the official language is Portuguese. The official language of most Latin American countries is Spanish. Brazilians speak Portuguese because Brazil was once a colony of Portugal. Explorer Pedro Álvares Cabral claimed Brazil for Portugal in 1500, and Portuguese colonists began to arrive in the 1530s. In 1822, Brazil declared itself independent from Portugal.

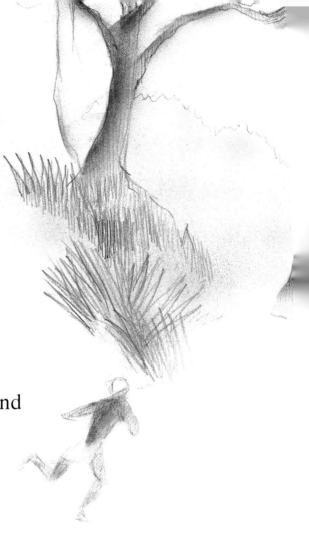

2 dois (DOH-eez)

There are **two** goals on a soccer field. In the fast-moving game of soccer, players use their feet, knees, hips, and even heads to move the ball down the field and into their opponents' goal. Soccer is one of the most popular sports in Brazil, where it is called *futebol* (foo-teh-BAHL). Maracanã Stadium in Rio de Janeiro (REE-oh day zhuh-NEH-roh) has long been the largest soccer stadium in the world. A Brazilian called Pelé, whose real name is Edson Arantes do Nascimento, is probably the most famous soccer player in history.

Other popular sports in Brazil include horse racing, waterskiing, hang gliding, and *capoeira* (kah-poh-AY-ruh), a sport found nowhere else. *Capoeira* is a fight, a dance, and a display of judo all in one. It dates back to the days of slavery. Slaves were punished if they were caught fighting, so they cleverly disguised their fights by pretending they were dancing instead of fighting.

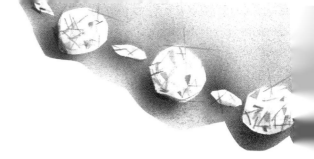

3 três (TRAY-ees)

Three important goods that made Portuguese colonists rich with the help of black slaves were sugarcane, diamonds, and gold. The Portuguese brought slaves from Africa—especially from the Portuguese colonies of Angola and Guinea—to grow sugarcane and to mine diamonds and gold. Slavery was abolished in Brazil in 1888. Over time, the former slaves and their descendants intermarried with the Europeans and native Indians. Modern Brazilian culture shows African influences in many areas, including cooking, sports, crafts, and music.

4 quatro (KWAH-troo)

Feijoada (fay-zhoh-AH-duh), the national dish of Brazil, is usually served at lunch on Saturdays. This thick stew contains many different ingredients, including black beans, beef, and pork. *Feijoada* is traditionally served with **four** side dishes: white rice, finely shredded kale, orange slices, and *farofa* (fah-ROH-fuh), which is fried manioc flour.

Feijoada was originally an African dish. Other African-influenced foods used in Brazilian cooking include palm oil, bananas, coconut milk, and hot spices.

5 cinco (SEEN-koo)

Brazil is divided into **five** regions: the North, the Northeast, the Central West, the Southeast, and the South.

The North is Brazil's largest region, but it has the fewest people. It includes the Amazon River and much of the Amazon rain forest. The Northeast is the country's poorest region. This area was the first to be colonized by Europeans, who established great sugarcane farms there. Most of the people who live there now are descendants of slaves. The Central West has thick forests and a large wetland area called the Pantanal (pan-tuh-NAWL), which is home to a huge variety of wildlife. This region also contains the country's capital city, Brasília (bruh-ZIHL-yuh). The Southeast is the region with the most people. The beautiful Southeastern coastal city of Rio de Janeiro, which was Brazil's capital until 1960, draws many visitors every year. The South includes vast grasslands, many farms, and the spectacular Iguaçú (ee-gwuh-SOO) Falls on the border between Brazil and Argentina.

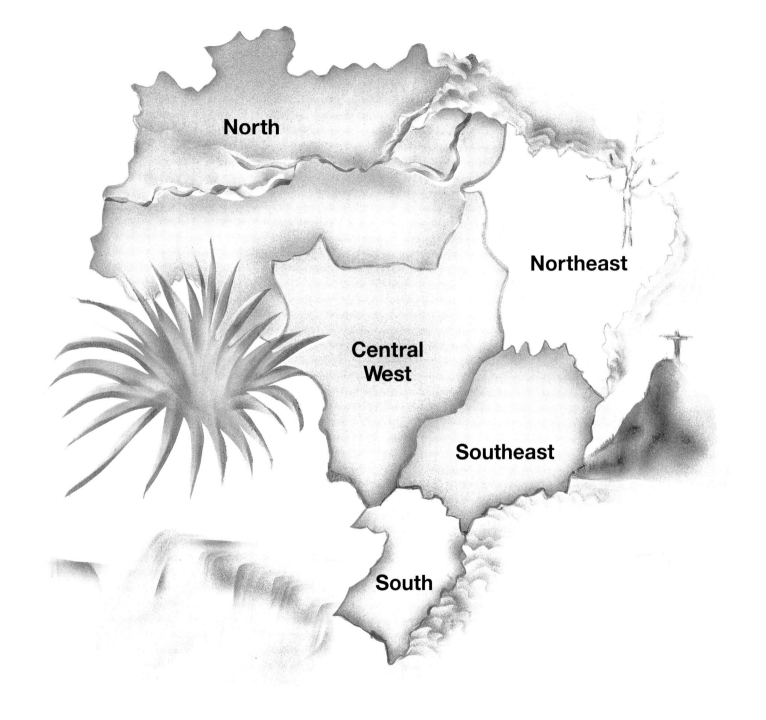

North

Northeast

Central West

Southeast

South

6 seis (SAY-ees)

The Feast of Iemanjá (ee-mahn-ZHAH) is celebrated every year on the beaches of Rio de Janeiro. **Six** gifts offered to the goddess Iemanjá are combs, flowers, fruit, hair ribbons, mirrors, and perfumes. Iemanjá was originally an African goddess of the sea. As slave religions combined with Catholicism, the religion of the Portuguese colonists, Iemanjá took on some qualities of the Virgin Mary. She became queen of the heavens as well as goddess of the sea.

7 sete (SEHT-chee)

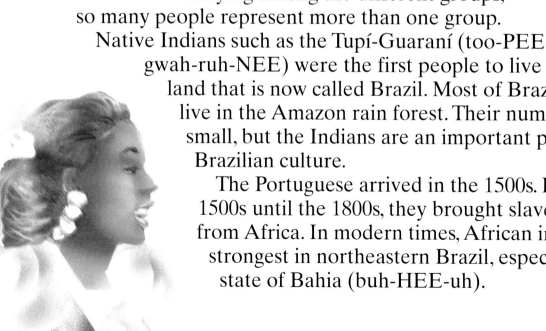

Seven different ethnic groups make up most of Brazil's population: native Indians, Portuguese, Africans, Italians, Spanish, Germans, and Japanese. There has been much intermarrying among the different groups, so many people represent more than one group.

Native Indians such as the Tupí-Guaraní (too-PEE gwah-ruh-NEE) were the first people to live on the land that is now called Brazil. Most of Brazil's Indians live in the Amazon rain forest. Their numbers are small, but the Indians are an important part of Brazilian culture.

The Portuguese arrived in the 1500s. From the 1500s until the 1800s, they brought slaves to Brazil from Africa. In modern times, African influence is strongest in northeastern Brazil, especially in the state of Bahia (buh-HEE-uh).

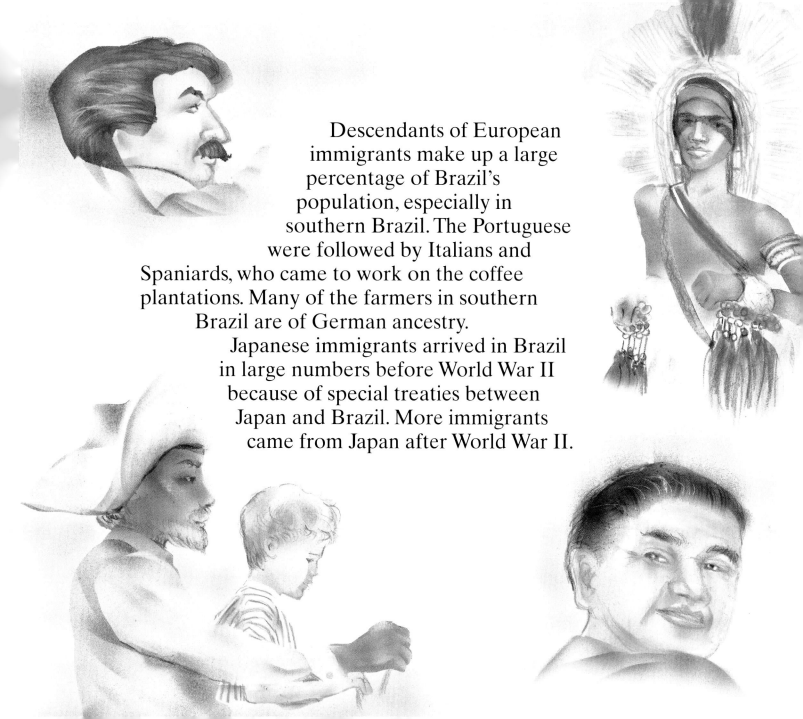

Descendants of European immigrants make up a large percentage of Brazil's population, especially in southern Brazil. The Portuguese were followed by Italians and Spaniards, who came to work on the coffee plantations. Many of the farmers in southern Brazil are of German ancestry.

Japanese immigrants arrived in Brazil in large numbers before World War II because of special treaties between Japan and Brazil. More immigrants came from Japan after World War II.

8 oito (OY-too)

Eight exotic animals of Brazil are armadillos, capybaras, tapirs, coatis, jaguars, two-toed sloths, manatees, and jabirus.

An armadillo looks more like a tank than an animal. It has an armorlike covering of bony plates. Both capybaras and tapirs look a bit like pigs. Capybaras are the world's largest rodents—adults are about four feet long and weigh more than 100 pounds. With their long snouts, tapirs may look like pigs, but they are actually related to horses and rhinoceroses. A coati looks like a raccoon with a longer snout and tail.

The jaguar, a large wildcat with a spotted coat, is known as a fierce hunter. The two-toed sloth, on the other hand, is said to be lazy. It spends hours hanging upside down from trees, eating leaves. Manatees are large water animals with two flippers and a flat, oval tail. Another Brazilian animal found near water is the jabiru, a large wading bird with white feathers.

nove (NOH-vee)

Nine important products of Brazil come from trees. Food products include cashews, Brazil nuts, oranges, papayas, and cacao beans (which are used to make chocolate). Trees also supply carnauba wax (which is used to make such things as polishes and carbon paper), medicines, latex (which is used to make rubber), and, of course, timber.

More than half of Brazil is covered with forests, much of it the Amazon rain forest. Even the name of the country came from a tree, the brazilwood, which was once used to make red dye.

10 dez (dehz)

Music is very important to the people of Brazil. **Ten** instruments used to play Brazilian music are guitars, triangles, accordions, clarinets, tall drums, maracas, harmonicas, ukuleles, banjos, and one-stringed bows called *berimbaus* (beh-rihm-BOHS). There are so many different kinds of instruments because Brazil's music, like its people, is so varied. Brazil's music comes from Africa, Europe, and the Caribbean, and from the Indians who were the land's first inhabitants.

Pronunciation Guide

1 / **um** / oong

2 / **dois** / DOH-eez

3 / **três** / TRAY-ees

4 / **quatro** / KWAH-troo

5 / **cinco** / SEEN-koo

6 / **seis** / SAY-ees

7 / **sete** / SEHT-chee

8 / **oito** / OY-too

9 / **nove** / NOH-vee

10 / **dez** / dehz